Sam Hickford

Littoral Press

First Published by
The Littoral Press, 15 Harwood Place,
Lavenham, Sudbury, Suffolk CO10 9SG

Illustration by Csenge Santa

ISBN 978-1-912412-33-4

British Library Cataloguing-in-Publication Data:
A catalogue record of this book is available from
The British Library

Printed and bound in Great Britain by
4Edge Ltd. Hockley, Essex
www.4edge.co.uk

Contents

First Journey: Moston

There is a perfect circle, if only now;
all real commuters turned to bus, or tram.
Only some industrious Hollingwood dealer scans
the full expanse of the unleavened boughs

that mark England's only cyclical motorway.
Just here, the orbit can be seen, the care
by horticulturalists & planners - the despair
of diesel particles swimming in array

mapping out this unholy miracle.
In one moment, cars will skim past the moss
and lichen, stampeding in their daily prowl

the stretch-marks of the circle as it swells.
In far too many years, everything humans embossed
will be erased. This is a perfect circle only now.

Todmordine Rite

Where the sorb is rattling, whipped by the wild
wind, and the hills; there, we have chosen a place
a tamed wolf can rest, among its elemental synergy,
among a straight-talking briar as its nest.

Brutal and blessed, the Labrador is dressed
in earth contusions. I am studying the hole
and watch it swallow all the newly-tressed
entrails of dog-bone, muted howl, and bracken.

This soul, flailing from its body, is the first thing
I remember, I swear, and so, our deaths are births
and you were there to officiate it all
and I said nothing, dog-mute in this dirge.

A Secret Garden I

The wasp would terrorise us out of its
unkempt & mortal beauty, goading us from
our childed bodies; tiny fingertips
spindled with moss, which led us to be one

with a little patch that blossoms round a skip
& she is ushering it. Badger-nested
stubble, primrose-peeks, & out-of-place
cowslip, not that a single one infected

the blotching surface of that rugged heaven
or tried to give the knotted brambles shape.

A Secret Garden II

Green is giving way to its impersonator,
a mock-utopian spray of tennis-bleach:

impassive likelihoods of English lawns, creating
the badgers' cold displacement. Here, each

scurries to a make-shift habitat
among the golf course or the stub of flats

& primroses perform their final sway
in hackneyed rituals they've had to learn

from meadowed land they're forced to turn away
& try to refuge from. This violent spring

continues; nascent flowers begin to shred
from human tool-work, clipping off the wings

they've worked their stems off to regenerate
& so the astroturf announces - *here*

I am, in crop circle arrogance & smoothed with hate
for the meadows it unfolded & upreared.

The Soul Speaks

and then I found a fickle man,
or would-be man, to burst into,
and tunneled through his fickle hands,
and carved his body into two;

and now I'm image of my host.
I am the weight of every flight.
I stretched the body from a ghost.
I am the beacon of its light

and then I found a lesser thing;
a mossy god beneath the earth,
I tried this trick again: my wings
snapped off before they beat to birth.

Now I'm the mouldywarp that sits
upon the absence of all sound.

Atlas (un)burdened

Once, I carried many worlds within my hands;
kernels created to excite the slate
of which we tire, with its atmospheric
landscape of heaving weightlessness. I prayed,

one night, and, as usual, put the pebbles where they stand
within their convoluted, imperfect mosaic.
But then I woke up - in the still-broken day -
and sold off every planetlet to the dodgiest bidder

all except one. And I love this as if my mind
or soul, as it grows up, as is the way of worlds:
and on its growing mass I concentrate
holding it upwards as a sacrifice.

(And, one day, yielding to its greater weight,
from this vantage point within the sky,
I will submit into a black hole in this slate
and take only the pulleys where I die.)

The Poet on Learning First Hand That There is A Plaque of John Clare in Peterborough Shopping Centre

Frankly, it is just absurd, and no
poem will ever do it any justice; the way his head
is inclosed above some local industrialist -
he who dwelled among the fens - & how
would he, himself, have articulated any of this?

Your temptation's to write about it as if him,
saying, you know, "the wood-gate led me to the blush
and so I passed the shop-rows entered Lush
where no thicket hath ever spiralled in
nor swamp invaded only a bath-bomb spins

upon a flaggy shelf vegan yet unnatural
but still the puddock faintly starts to trill"
Etc. But Clare's not here, only this morbid likeness
of him. I walked from Helpston, just now, camping in the eye
of a storm, and have spoken with his ghost. I know

Clare when I see him. He was in the lightning, not
in the A47, though I saw 'awes and clock-a-clays
along that thoroughfare... he was half-there,
murmuring in Swaddywell, but this plaque has killed John Clare
or fatally wounded him, through its affirmation

of him. Or does a snipe begin to wade
within the battered swamps where oceans aren't
or does a nightingale softly chant

upon an apple-tree upon an A1
roundabout? Hark! It's only half-over, now.

The Ark

(to a guy I "care for" who likes to dismantle furniture)

Yes, I have allowed you to demolish every slab,
hammer tables to pieces; but, for some reason,
I will not ever let you touch this raft.

Why? Some creature of possibility
compels me to imagine that I'll have to save
two perfect members of humanity

and I'd have something to quickly help you into,
and him, and then the deluge would assault,
so please do not destroy this part of you.

when you

whirled
with me
in the

monastery
i thought:
finally

this
not that
is love
-rumi kaur

To An Ex-Pupil at Cathedral Academy

Of course, poetry is stupid, pretentious, & you're completely right,
there isn't any reason for the breaks, after every single
line - it isn't natural. And - thank fuck - you actually admit this,
not like 11(1), who revellingly take the piss
out of me, who cares about this whole pretentious thing
like that twat you fought, who said the way caesurae sing
into the "silence of the page", is like the "thunderstorm
of bullets", tearing up our "militaristic norms"
of "twentieth century" "society". Bastard. I'm sort of glad,
even as a pacifist, that you chose to twat

him, caesuraelessly. I know that you can get that joke,
have enough intelligence to, though you probably won't
ever see this. I loved the way you came to class,
stoned out of your mind, and curiously asked
every thing you'd ever wished to know
within my single-cactused, black-as-Wakefield coal
classroom (if you could ever call it that.)
I loved the way you only ever sat
truly focused, & of course you never wrote
anything down, or did a single piece of work

like Socrates. I forgave you when I met
you; your dad was dying, and so I read
a poem that I sort of wrote for Amber.
Your apathy (for work) escaped. A candour
intoxicated you. And all this is unrecorded,
obviously, in the mock exam, which you aborted

because you worked out the whole thing was bollocks.
Because of Covid, your grade is based on this. A product,
no doubt, of a curious life. You will veer far astray
from poetry. I hope we meet again some day.

East Lancashire Railway

Later - as an adult - I actually *got* that train
that stormed under our feet, as we tried - our best - to feign
(or, I did), that we knew how to smoke. I held the flame,

unburning, as that train outcoughed us, warbling
in lungless steaming wheezes, burrowing its antique wings
into that indifferent town. I bought packs of Superkings

because I liked the name. Later, I had forgotten
this spot. Then my family and I took it to Ramsbottom,
that vintage railway, which, overlooking, we had plotted

our entire lives - or the shadows of them - in the ash
not only literally, but in the stubbornly-operating ruins of the past
(and, bearing in mind, I'm pretty sure this was the last

trip me and my sister went on, before she slipped
off, herself, into the smog-song. But that's immaterial.) This
is for you, and that poem that you hissed

into the black-pudding-scented yarrow, yearning,
bereaved yet adolescent, into the softly burning
swollen organ of the town we left, to which I am returning

here, recreating every rhythm of every private
whorl of word-dizzy dialogue, and punctuated silence
as the blueprint of my life. What quiet

endlessness have we woven from these moments?
What life is given to a pair of loners
whose loneliness is only intimacy, unspoken
in the rattle of that never-dying vintage train?

Ada Lovelace's Computer

I have studied a perfect blueprint for a living thing.
I am compelled to maintain its ingenuity, and then compelled, in turn, to proclaim an absolute inanimation.
I mean that it is just a frozen clockwork
for a universe that isn't living
despite its flawnessness and cold perfection.

And so, having studied the Analytical Machine,
I plotted a kind of resuscitation, entreating
the sprockets to begin to speak to one another
(for they are poised so perfectly in place.)
I imagine languaging every lever, breathing
into the flowerets of steam-fuelled meshes

but this is partial. This is paragenesis.
The world was never ready to be alive.

On Running Naked on a Golf Course (York, 2015)

After the predicted liberation, it is oddly mundane,
in fact. As if this is a tired old sport
like pétanque, played by confirmist Druid kids
intoxicated with their mainstream divinity

  classes. I think of mysticism: being winged in flight
like a golf-ball, from a blackbird's quivered beak
is a later extrapolation. It is the hard grind
beyond metaphor that counts, not this laboured hole-in-oneness.

Second Journey: The Dotted Line

In this phantasmagoria
the scars of vehicles open up like wounds
and there are poems to be plucked, but each
one bleeds on to the dashboard, or collides
against the bonnet in an 80 mph
crosswind, and I try to stop
and dance all their collisions into place.

At West Norwood Cemetery

Cerberus:
  a non-biodegradable coffee cup,
    guardian of the recently-deceased.

  I lay plastic wreaths upon your grave.
    These, too, will outlive you.

Galapagos Elegies

I: Saudi gazelle

The brook is faint
 that I have pined for. But I wore its mirage.
  Wove it, wrapped it across my silken skin

and shared it with my tribe. And then I cantered,
 following the desert's underside
  and chased the sun, delirious of worship.

And here and there the saltbush torments me
 with all the viscera that dreams can bear,
  bleeding through the outline of my hide.

The waters kill that I have chased along
 Iram. But they also cry with love,
  bearing the pain of life. And so I yearn,
   here and there, for the nourishment of sand.

II: Baiji dolphin

A circlet of us
  gathered, in the flowering
    spine-length, where the dam is
      lain, heralding with tiny eyes,
        and flagged fins, the exhaustible blue
          artery of Yangtze.

I will reconvene the school
  along the corridor, clothed in a mass
    of oil-spilled blubber, before my flukes fold into
      fossils, in the spume of cargo.

III: Bramble cay meloyms

I scuttled:
  a leaf of nypa-palm
    vesselled to a new land,
      and then I whispered, foraging
        in dark hog-weed. Winds came
          and cradled sea-birds in their
            arms. I stayed here.

From the unmoving boat, while I sleep,
 my mosaic whiskers are woven in what bore me;
   my scurry is a song-within-the-wave
     and for one minute the scuttler
       submerges, and I whimper one stroke
         of resistance.

IV: The golden toad

Drags of forest-rain boulder, then wash
away the folds of my blanket: a whited cape
sewn around my body like curse. A boy

with treasure girdled around his amphibian
limbs turns out to be a brute. Sharp blades
of monsoon are coming far too late, then far too soon -

my chosen lover is this shawl of rain, an uncommon
preciousness, in the depths of a gown of trees.
I lie with him, waiting for the world to end.

V: Pyrenean ibex

My tongue is crooked
and I would have bleated, singing
on the mountains that up-held my withers
and I will never see.

My heart is fire
and I would have over-heated, clinging
to my hircine husband (any will do -), beside
the silver-fir, or against the scrawl of pine.

My mind is blooming
and I would have had repose, among
a carpet of grass, upon which
I would have dreamt together blankets of leaves.

Though I am ghost
although I know that ghosts can live again
undead for seven minutes, on which they climb
and scale the promontories which they left.

My lungs are failing
and I would have breathed in every beam of air,
breathed in every rock within the sky.

VI: Pinta Island tortoise

Under my scutes, there are written stories
that I forgot to tell, kept to myself.
I carried an entire world upon my back

which I yielded, painlessly, to my only predator,
as a manuscript for an unpublished map
of meditations in a secret century.

Motorway Bridge

(in memoriam Laurian Bold)

The sky is a lesson plan
blue black, stretched over
an artery of noise.

I have lived too much,
in the background of closet
spaces, sleepless years.

Somebody is interrupting:
a whispered, silenced "no"
in a network of veins.

This is not mythic,
it is GCSE physics:
acceleration, inertia.

Il Megabus, Mont-Blanc

1
within the spaces affective where disappear even words and sense * into the clouds of pollution we have fathomed * there is a split second moment in which l'inquinamento può essere... guardato... come bello... in cui la natura che abbiamo macchinata è la sola cosa bella... in which, bewitched, the stubborn * water beckons into the tauntfully-glistening fortress - * dove cantano le fate e i gobline d'antan, into the glistening wordsworth-walked forest *, et - croyez-moi, j'ai essayé - tant j'ai essayé - à parlare con te... * bien que je ne t'aie que rencontré il y a un momento... a Megabus second, in other words, within which, and on the back of which, we have covered such emotional and physical distance... et * maintenant - quelle vanité! - nous avons reçu cette image épauliale ce dont il s'agit - tout s'en agit - although we shouldn't - although la notte è una montana - che ci ingoia, e ora ci ha ingoiato... che già ci ha ingoiato * therefore - and this goes without saying, really - which tongue will catalyse the after-reality of this space, which tongue * beckons water into la fortezza d'oro infinito. which one? La mia bella straniera, la mia bella* strainer, ascolta la mia preghiera, perché noi (malgré une certaine manque d'intimité, qui, bien sûr, est perpetuelle), noi moriremo cui. Noi

2
moriremo da qualche parte come cui, credo di sì; or, at the very least, in the same sea, among and languishing within the imprints of an oil-black pollution, with only the toxic waves to spell out our name, senza fine

3

so, where, then, are we now? I don't know, really, but io ti amo tantissimo, e what distances have we covered, cowered along, and sprawled, within the vacuum of our closeness, and why, after all, abbiamo bisogno della distanza per rivelare la nostra cuore - (non, je dis aux autres; laissez-nous, je vous prie, notre solitude imparfaite, bien que vous soyez si proche, vous pouvez toujours être lointains, je pense, et ta langue aussi, je voudrais déchirer de ma gorge, cette langue, je veux dire, juste une fois...) e la nostra cuore sta fiorendo... et le ninfe della collina e del cielo dansano, ancora, tra il profumo della benzina. So let's watch the sky, let's watch the waves skirt the industrious surface, watch'd by the flames of chiaro di luna. Let us love the spaces affective, which lie between us, where disappear even words and sense.

Familiar Tissue

"My father is given to me and I dissect his body. I study him carefully. You ask me where I learn anatomy?" - Stanislaw Szukalski

As every sinew, tendon, lies apart
I reflect that only, in these loving scrapes
will he be at all remembered, in the throes of art

where I will sew him up in wondrous shapes:
a sculpture of a pair of disembodied feet.
A sculpture of a knee. A bronze of splayed

flesh. After this nightmare, I find my dad complete
and undissectable, with an unsutured heart
and, in a sleepwalk, I cut up the sheet.

Three Islands

I – Monastery

"And you would do that - lock yourself away
intentionally?" Equally, I could demand the yew tree why

it might be efficacious to grow, and afterwards decay

within these mirrors of silence; why choose to hide
yourself among the bindweed? Almost sentiently
the tree pipes up, just as I began to confide
in its imagined spirit. "Why did you come here intentionally?"

II – School

This hallucination grows back on some usual jagged day
at work, you know; I'm so bored I wander by

the panopticon that the school deems "Isolation", some bye-way

into criminality. I watch kids almost conditioned to defy
the Student Liaison Officer, a hungover sentinel
as if to provoke them into that common spiral
into prison. It is done intentionally

& prematurely. Now isolation is our only cliché;
a God who takes us on an involuntary ride
to twat us if we don't meditate or pray.

They are parsing open, surgically, our eyes
to mourn an old self's death. Uncryptically
the yew tree flowers, lanky in undemise
while we are locked away intentionally.

Obituarying...

...using the present continuous,
Not the imperfect:

We are living
She is dying
They are making

something, something or other, some wholly
pretty terror, from the nervous alchemy
of birth and unbirth, how they are coming
together, how one simply miscarries oneself
eventually, from the womb we have the gall
to still inhabit. *We are mourning*

forever - I think you know! - and cannot now
unknow - for I am making a vivisection
of the past...

this is too much, too whirlwinding, and I am
getting that which I deserve, an endlessness, a
startlessness, and see
you resurrecting and becoming new
you desiccating and becoming...

all in one motion, one unmotion, where nowt
and all marry like those fatal little twins
from old, I mean from now, we cannot stop,
we only still ourselves, the mind revolves,

we go and then we stop, but never rest.
I am resting. There is no heaven here, you know.
The womb will usher us, and off we go.

Three Airports

I: Manchester Airport
(for Rahul Gupta, the proper poet)

A terminus: a plover alights upon a fir
On Hringhaeg's ancient runway. West Valley's that: a rill
still shrieking. For a second, that plover's still
before that call is wrenched from out of her
winged in winter fog and furrowed chill.
Well, here's me, yearning, dreaming her return
to these brumous forests: perhaps a flight from Bern,
Bangkok? Those sounds are flushing out the rill
and swill and storm the stop-gap of the stern
of this too-beaten boat. Swirling in the haze
is an assembly trembling out in praise
in downward spirals: I cannot hear her in that blur.
Try to forget, I know. Still, I stay until
a blotted star is straining to emerge
among the rain, the white-black waves. It's her
gone quiet a second: calling, distant, still.

II: Leeds-Bradford Airport

…a bone-white plough. her beak
over rides one “brinded cow” (liveried in white & brown.) she surges, surges. she mounts the boundary stones, emerging, merging with mist &
ploughs the cotton-mill clouds. the Celts lie deep, sleeping in concrete...
...now, her winded-wound crest beams her into the self-same shroud They gestured to. (you imagine processions of red & white.)
carbonic incense tapers down…
…that deaf-grazing cow, behind
barbed-wire-boundary-stone, has a moment of respite: a briared river’s flow’s brown & white, in moon-of-evening’s hushed-up light…
…wild-fowl: they whimper
wearied moon-wet lullabies. their home’s a nearby
Dam quite drowned in the drone of ryanairs bleating across t’ Aire...
…a Tesco bag braves the
cross-wind. it’s abstract now: its plough-songs
of white-of-bone.

III: Newcastle Airport

A horse & carriage croodles past - half-sees a solitary oak
enwrapped in ringlet-growths of grass enveloping as altar-stones
&, then, a swash of swimmers spreads
these stretch-marks on a limber lake
& gilliflowers garlic juts along the road where cars now race
besides a railway, hollowed-out, wi' cowslips & wi' butterflies
that carries low-speed passengers along its mythic-motioned line;
they flutter in the allocated corridors of perfumed shade
dwarfed soon enough by rollercoasters,
threshing in the meadowed plains
& human figures in this landscape -
hauntings? - swaddle in the hay
fallen in a Viking conquest, ejected from an aeroplane;
and now & then a living person slouches from a caravan
or dog-walks (always!) through the vallum
by the Northumbrial land.

A Burial Corridor

"Surely what is needed now is a grand strategic vision for green burial places to reclaim our cities with urban and peri-urban woods and forests and for it to be a requirement for trunk transport routes to include linear wildlife burial corridors alongside them" – Professor John Ashton, 'Necropolis in crisis', *Journal of the Royal Society of Medicine.*

Is there a better way to see you off
than amidst the screeching and the hum
of wheedling engines, feistily gobbling
automated fuel? There is no better. I remember
hirpling over the dream-M62
past crop-circles. Past cottages and cotton-clouds
& you in the passenger-seat. I felt you breathe
against the dashboard & I reckoned that
somehow I'd clawed a road into your heart
(or, at least, some blocked-off artery…)

They grew an oak tree. Day by day, it guides –
miniature – the frantic traffic through the road
burdened with busy prayers & sacred sights
& burdened with my deaf-drone pilgrimage
among the whiplash-sky and metal-rain.
There is no better. God or this guide has seated you
among a gas-leak meadow in the stars.

Third Journey: Salford Viaduct

In an early drawing, its archways are in perfect harmony
with every little house and leaping ash -

mosaic of symmetric brick: one angel crashed
in swarming fog, and many died, but Thee

have served us well, in general, fair portals
of Jerusalem! We are Sat Nav guided through you.

John Clare on the Tube

Frit by the crankling train that storms the brigs
of Harrow clock-a-clays & woven twigs
are soodling passengers - theyre sleeping tight
clothéd in rawky natures faded light
& younkers maul & lease their mothers love
as sprents the sweat, 'mid echoes from above.

I love to watch the Tube sturt in the night
bosoming the lowns within its airy flight
across the elting in its grassy sleep
besomed by suthying men. Then in one creep
sturt hinging Smartphoneers & startling men
& well-clout women begin their 'Jobs' again.

A Road Somewhere in Preston

we might as well say that King Arthur rode
along this thoroughfare. diademed & many-menned.
just as - for certain - Roman soldiers, droves
of regiments, spaced like a cattle-load
daubed certain slabs of roadwork crimson-red.
though each one - private... - walked this stretch of road
one or two forgetting that it was their "own"
from time to time. or future-dreams of living deaths
made them lose their lode. but generals drove

them onwards. so this Sat Nav, keeled by code
bleeps fierce instructions like a general
at every mitsubishi on the road
regardless of its status: young & old
& dutied flat-capped veterans are sent
to the same watering-points in cattledroves
on Roman Roads: car-parks outside Tesco's
where £20 will nab a sacrament.
but yellow-lined, pot-holed, this still must be the Road
which ancients (!) set upon and, absent, drove.

Preston Bus Station

"Who on earth boasts about having the second biggest of anything, let alone something as unsexy as a bus stop?" - Lancashire Post.

A monument to The Journey's Absolute
Baroque triumph against the petty times & spaces
it is supposed to consist of. Look, most terminals are mute
ruins of ancient routes no more existent: Morecambe Bay
via Lancaster, we imagine. But now, an unserviced fugue
into ghost-villages now suburbed: shiny, enticing bays
that carry nowhere but to themselves. Though those remaining

interchange & this obsesses you. Maps & charts. Not place
itself, just movement's curious tango: the way each bus is totally
consumed within the rhythm of its signature. A patterned whole
remains but no close-quartered bus will scrape another. Fumes
whirligig in salmon-pink-tinting skies. Before this haze
nothing connects. Similarly, I & you

are imprisoned within the wing-mirror of our monomaniacal
gazes:
lonely pre-signalled routes. Morecambe & Wise: "Make
me happy, through the years" is the thought that chortles through
your mind, a song I've never heard: a half-remembered Blake
pretentiously levels through mine. & though it's true
I've learnt the song by the way you simulate
its vocal wrangles, & can sing with you on cue

(& you know 'London'...) after this the routes have changed

& fail to intersect. I leave you or you leave me. &, straight,
I hulk over far-distant roads, & the exalted few
moments we relate have disintegrated. (Even-weirded fate
is of master-forged stainless steel.) As the path assails, any news
grows fainter. Where did you go? The map erased your name
forever, as the well-wrought rota, once static;
the paper-thick truth
of horaria, chartered realities that a tattered page
lays host to. & altered, tattered scraps so much outgrew
the Sunshine. Even so, every thing is interchange

and this explains - I suppose - why that awful café
serving hash browns, bad coffee, is so much estranged
yet near. Of all places! Everything, everything is interchange

On Rivers & Pandemics

1350

It was not saintly cunning, nor a flare
leaping around the long-chilled heart. Nor logic,
really. A straightforward instinct drew Pierre
not to half-unify just yet with God
in the celestial realm. Facsimiles of prayer

from experts led them to prescribe a torch
commanding him to wield it every day.
He practised - *Ave Maria, Gratia Plena, Dominus Tecum*
with a spear of straw, to chase the moon away
which the Devil had engineered in the sky

to shape-shift, unlike that monoformal sun.
Yet - noticing, if he just kept himself
from touching gestures, embraces with the Avignon
faithful - Pierre felt himself protected
without the savageness of real light, shone

to burn infection. Bolted up in the studium
of the Palais des Papes, remembering his half-arsed
monkishness, which roan or hunting-dog in the fresco stunned
bim into self-endangerment? Self-isolating, Clement VI -
this time, a real Pope - feels the evangelium's

fervour drip into his ear. He thinks of every unburied
peasant, dying without pardon, forgiving every last soul's
faintest flicker of venial sin. There's a General Absolution,

(& all this when forgiveness could be bought or sold
in shops) although, the ocean of death is inundating

Pierre's archipelago of self-isolation.

Socially distant (this is easy, anyway; believers are marshalled
from the sanctuary), Pierre carefully consecrates
the entire Rhone, as the graveyards overflow
with spirits, clamouring for some more efficacious
2020
disposal. No, that is absolute nothing,
at all, like this. Well, even so, the entire river
is suddenly awakened; just as those who suddenly
quicken to their slumber are delivered
into the fatal origin, suddenly exposed.

This is nothing like that; though, we too lost a priest
or two, & when we try to speak or whisper into
its core, it will be with a newer mouth.
I am listening to the New River. It tunnels through
the boisterous, feisty silence, as if we only ever slept

before, though we were inammorate of noisy
vortexes - bars that now are barricaded shut -
the city is unclothed. A faded voice...
I am listening to the New River; it cuts
across new London, as shards of ivy, poised

along its real flow actually sway
in living & subsident mystery
lying within a point within a rill.
It is impossible to quantify entirely

the misery, I know; the blackbird's trill
ignites a painful, resurrected Europe.

Distance

Heaven is Pandemic - of Pandemos - earthly-
eternally immersed in our images of it. Heaven
rises, in other words, in the smoke-song of mundane
liquid-amber gleams of tea - especially - it forms

angels of one-moment condensations
huddled together, in the apparition
that I daily conjure, as a structured
miracle. I watch it leap

into the atmosphere of the room
and settle in the tracery of chairs
and canvases of windows, mourning it
as a croak of wind, or a particle of air.

A Willow-Tree, in Hiroshima

Softly & impossibly, her roots still beckon
growth. It is a slow hope she is drawing.

Their ends were swift - echoes in the floorboards.
I am reliving it, since I am solitary.

A thrawning suffocation grabs the sky
so gradually. *Not yet*, I said, *not yet*.

In W H Smith

(to my sister, Amber)

Each bronze, or silver, gel pen, is
ammunitioned only for a moment's scribble...
(a moment's struggle with the equally
too smooth or inauthentic paper, which
burdens several aisles, as if to paradox
the struggle between the nothing and the
overwrought,) and buried deep within the un-
used cartridgery, is an unwritten novel, which,
against your first advice, I have given
away the villain's whole identity:
a simple cluster of particles, assembled
in some disfigured vision of a fate
(which cannot be un-clotted or un-incubated
and is still sleeping on within its host
or in the ungenerated stationery
you covet, coveted, sort of like a magpie?, not
for its execution, but the potential it allows;
plastic boxes bearing measuring
implements, calculators, using which
you did too little. And me.
But, well, this is your temple -
and so I try to stencil out a prayer
with a stolen pen, among the busy hirelings,
energetic with post-covid-
nineteen-jitters.) The staff polish the emotion away.

Funeral Song

after Paul Élouard

People leave their bodies. & horses gallop on
& stop and rest. The door will just not open
by itself. The noisest birds turn quiet. Their sweet songs
don't go with them to the grave. &, yet again,

the tree is shaken. The butterflies still on the branch
feel so deeply that the winter comes, will come
so soon. So we wait, patiently, and hang
just here, to be with her, & never reach the sun.

But I really need to ask. Why is this wilted flower
still crying? Why do these lilies seem to sing?
& - tell me! - what about this rose of amber -
which is growing endlessly and tender?

Fine. They had to hide her in the ground.
So why can we still hear her, deafeningly loud?
Because she's here, she's here.